THE CHILDREN'S BOOK OF
AMERICA

EDITED BY

William J. Bennett

ILLUSTRATED BY

Michael Hague

SCHOLASTIC INC.

New York Toronto London Auckland Sydney
Mexico City New Delhi Hong Kong Buenos Aires

THE CHILDREN'S BOOK OF
AMERICA

ISBN 0-439-45855-2

12 11 10 9 8 7 6 5 4 3 2   2 3 4 5 6 7/0

Printed in the U.S.A.   24

First Scholastic paperback printing, September 2002

Designed by Amy Hill

CONTENTS

*To Dorothy and Clarence, Nancy, Lois
and F. Robert, who taught Elayne and
me to love our country*
—W.J.B.

To Hopalong Cassidy
—M.H.

INTRODUCTION

Our Founding Fathers knew that a democracy flourishes only when its citizens cherish certain ideals and will not let them go. Love of liberty and equality. Faith in the Almighty. Attention to the cultivation of character. Respect for truth. Pride in good work. These are the kinds of principles that make America great, and if we are to stay great, we must raise our children to love them. Lessons about national character are taught in several ways: by the examples adults offer, by the expectations we set for youngsters, by the laws citizens obey, by the customs people honor. The spirit of America also comes alive for children in stories from our past. This book tells a handful of those stories with the aim of teaching young hearts and minds about some of our best ideals and aspirations.

In these pages, children meet some of the historical events, legends, songs, and poems that are their legacy. Abigail Adams, amid confusion and bloodshed, calmly takes up a pen to sustain her husband and their dream of independence. Lewis and Clark stand at the forks of the Missouri River and study its waters intently, knowing that somewhere upstream lies a nation's destiny. John Henry's hammer whirls like the wind and falls like a thunderclap, each stroke announcing that the American spirit *will* prevail. These episodes and images supply us with a sense of self as a nation, telling us who we are, where we come from, what we are about. They are part of what Abraham Lincoln called the "mystic cords of memory" that bind us together as a people.

When children hear of the Pilgrims at Plymouth, they learn about the love of freedom that led to this country's founding. In the story of our national anthem, they see that our forefathers had to stand fast in defense of liberty. In tales of the Civil War or the civil rights movement, they learn how long it took to extend that liberty to all Americans. When we share these stories with children, we teach them about the ideals we revere, the principles by which we want them to live. And thus we welcome them to a common American culture.

In introducing youngsters to their heritage, we should not hesitate to tell stories of heroes and heroines and thrilling adventure. Davy Crockett at the Alamo. Abe Lincoln splitting rails on the frontier. The world holding its breath while it waits for the words "The *Eagle* has landed." These stories ring with high drama and inspiration, and they win the hearts of children. Too often the modern day disposition is to take the heroism and poetry—the romance—out of our accounts of America. This shortchanges our young, because in truth the great story of America is filled to the brim with heart-stirring drama. As the historian Bernard DeVoto wrote:

> *If the mad, impossible voyage of Columbus or Cartier or La Salle or Coronado or John Ledyard is not romantic, if the stars did not dance in the sky when our Constitutional Convention met, if Atlantis has any landscape stranger or the other side of the moon any lights or colors or shapes more unearthly than the customary homespun of Lincoln and the morning coat of Jackson, well, I don't know what romance is. Ours is a story mad with the impossible, it is by chaos out of a dream, it began as dream and it has continued as dream down to the last headlines you read in a newspaper. . . . The simplest truth you can ever write about our history will be charged and surcharged with romanticism.*

If this collection conveys a sense of such grand adventure, it is in no small measure because of Michael Hague's own vision of that magical place called America. It was Michael who first suggested this book, and his brush, as always, beckons children into the stories. In these pages, it also opens their eyes to the beauty and goodness of this great country.

The story of America is, after all, a hopeful story. At times it has been faltering and uneven. But in the end, ours is a story of triumph. This really is, as the songs say, the land of the noble free, the place of the patriot dream that sees beyond the years, the home of heroes who, more than self, their country love. I hope this book helps us celebrate our unparalleled story. May it also help us share with our children the remarkable spirit of America.

"America the Beautiful"

— KATHARINE LEE BATES

A teacher named Katharine Lee Bates wrote this beautiful hymn in 1893 after seeing her country from atop snow-capped Pike's Peak in Colorado. She firmly believed that America's glory would last only as long as we crown its greatness with goodness, and its bounty with brotherhood.

 beautiful for spacious skies,
For amber waves of grain,
For purple mountain majesties
Above the fruited plain!
America! America!
God shed His grace on thee,
And crown thy good with brotherhood
From sea to shining sea!

O beautiful for Pilgrim feet,
    Whose stern, impassioned stress
A thoroughfare for freedom beat
    Across the wilderness!
America! America!
    God mend thine every flaw,
Confirm thy soul in self-control,
    Thy liberty in law!

O beautiful for heroes proved
    In liberating strife,
Who more than self their country loved,
    And mercy more than life!
America! America!
    May God thy gold refine,
Till all success be nobleness
    And every gain divine!

O beautiful for patriot dream
    That sees beyond the years,
Thine alabaster cities gleam
    Undimmed by human tears!
America! America!
    God shed His grace on thee,
And crown thy good with brotherhood
    From sea to shining sea!

The Legend of the Grand Canyon

Scientists say it took millions of years for the Colorado River to cut through a mile of rock and form the Grand Canyon. The Indians of the Southwest tell a different tale about the origins of this vast geological wonder.

In the dry, rugged country of the American West there once lived a great Indian chief. His wife was a wise and kind woman who filled his heart with happiness. They loved each other so deeply that anyone who saw them together could not help but smile. But one day the wife was bitten by a rattlesnake and departed this earth even before the sun went down.

The chief was a brave man, but he was not ready for this loss. Now there was no joy in his life, and he could do nothing but wander the land mourning for his wife. So deep was his sorrow that all of nature seemed to share it. The flowers bent their heads in despair. The stars dimmed in the sky. The birds left off their singing.

His people, too, felt his loss and grieved with him. No longer did they tend their crops or go hunting and fishing. Their fires sank low. They forgot their songs and dances. The village stood silent and sad.

When the Great Spirit saw the effects of so much sorrow, he sent his messenger to comfort the chief.

"Courage," the Spirit Messenger said. "Your wife is happy in the Land of the Spirits. When your work on earth is done, you will join her there. Until then, she wishes you to do your duty to your people, for they need your guidance, and are hard-pressed by your neglect."

"If my wife is truly happy, let me see her!" the chief pleaded. "If I can know she is at peace, I will be able to live without her until my own time has come."

Because there was still much work for this good man to do on earth, the messenger agreed to take him to the Land of the Spirits so that he could witness his wife's bliss.

The journey to the spirit world led across a savage terrain. The way was blocked by giant mesas that reached past the horizons and buttes that jutted into the sky. No human could scale such a wall. So the Great Spirit carved a wide, deep opening through the highlands and beckoned the chief to enter. At the bottom of this measureless chasm he found a narrow, winding trail, which he knew he was to follow.

The chief set out on the path, which no other mortal had tread. Around him towered the steep walls of the gorge. Sometimes they shone bright red in the sun; at other times they took soft purple hues or turned gray with the shadows of passing clouds. In places the cliffs vaulted so high they obscured the sky itself and shut out all light. Then the chief walked in darkness and lost track of the days and nights.

A long, long way he traveled. Many times, weary and footsore, he thought of turning back. But remembering his grief, he always pushed on. At last he came to the Land of the Spirits, and there he saw his lost love.

She smiled at him, and he saw that she was happy. Once again his own heart was filled with joy. As his grief departed, he remembered the people he had left behind. He saw the silent village, the dying fires, the withered crops. He knew his tribe needed his wisdom and guidance and that he should be at home.

Back through the deep canyon the chief hurried. Now the winding trail seemed not so long and rough, for he traveled with a new resolve. He knew that someday he would rejoin his wife. Until that time, he would strive to be worthy of her by doing his duty to his people. He returned to his village, where he ruled wisely and kindly the rest of his life.

But now the way to the Land of Spirits stood open so that people might go there whenever they pleased. Such was not the wish of the Great Spirit. For every mortal has work to do in this life and is called to that happy World Beyond only when his duties have been performed.

And so the Great Spirit sent a wild and thundering river to cover the footpath in the bottom of the gorge. To this day the river rushes across boulders and against sheer cliffs, hiding the trail so that no living beings may find the Land of the Spirits. But the mighty Grand Canyon itself remains, and all who see it are struck with awe.

The Pilgrims and
the First Thanksgiving

America was founded by women and men who came to these shores lifting their eyes toward heaven.

In England four hundred years ago there lived a group of people we now call the Pilgrims. Their lives were not happy because they were not allowed to worship God the way they chose. When they tried to pray in their own way, they were thrown into prison or driven from their homes and jobs. Finally, in 1620, they could bear it no longer. Leaving all they loved behind, they boarded a small ship called the *Mayflower* and ventured out to sea. Perhaps they could practice their faith in that vast, far-off wilderness called America.

For two long hard months the Pilgrims crossed the stormy Atlantic Ocean. The *Mayflower* pitched and shook. Its beams groaned and its sides leaked. Men, women, and children grew ill. But at last they arrived in the New World. They came ashore, fell on their knees, and thanked God for bringing them across the wide and furious waters.

At once they began the business of founding their colony. First they built a large house for common use. Then they built smaller houses for each family. They named the village New Plymouth after the city in England from which they had set sail.

It was the heart of winter, and Plymouth Colony was in for a harsh, cruel beginning. The Pilgrims shivered in freezing winds and driving rains as they struggled to build their huts. The earth froze hard. Food was scarce—every night they wondered if there would be enough to eat the next day. And always they knew the Indians were watching. They heard their whoops and calls through the woods and saw smoke rising from their fires.

Then came the sickness. Many of the Pilgrims grew weak from lack of food and warmth. They lay in their beds, coughing and gasping for breath. Sometimes only a handful of settlers were well enough to cook and care for all the sick. Half the company died that long first winter. As the living buried their dead, they prayed and wondered if coming to America had not been a tragic mistake. But still they placed their faith in God.

Winter passed. The icy earth softened. One March day, as the settlers stared in wonder, a lone Indian strolled calmly into Plymouth, raised his hand, and cried "Welcome!" In broken English he told the Pilgrims his name was Samoset. He had learned their language from English fishermen who had visited the shores of the New World. He told them that the Indians who lived nearby were called the Wampanoags and were ruled by a wise chief named Massasoit.

A few days later Massasoit himself strode into Plymouth village with several of his braves. The Pilgrims spread a rug on the floor of an unfinished house and invited their visitors to sit. They ate and drank and talked together. They promised to live as neighbors and signed a treaty that kept peace between the two peoples for many years.

Massasoit brought with him an Indian named Squanto who spoke English. The settlers were amazed to hear this man's story. He had once been kidnapped by a sea captain and taken to Europe to be sold as a slave. Making his way to London, he had lived several years in the Pilgrims' own homeland before sailing back to the New World with English explorers.

It was Squanto who now stayed with the Pilgrims and helped them learn how to live in this strange, wild land. He showed them how to plant corn. He taught them how to

fish, and catch eels in the rivers, and dig in the mud for clams. He taught them how to hunt for deer in the forests. He showed them which berries were good to eat and which ones would make them sick. If not for Squanto's wisdom and aid, the little Plymouth colony may well have vanished.

Summer came. In the warm weather the Pilgrims grew stronger. With stout hearts they went to work in their fields and gardens. God blessed the land with sunshine and showers. The men and women of Plymouth watched the crops push up through the soil and prayed, for they knew they could not make it through the next winter without a good harvest.

The growing season passed and the days grew shorter. Fruit ripened. The pumpkins swelled orange and round. Autumn came in a blaze of glory, dressing the forests in gold and red and brown. The Pilgrims gathered the harvest, stored their food, and prepared themselves for the long, cold months that lay ahead.

They had much to be thankful for. The corn had grown well. The rivers and woods teemed with fish and game. The little houses were finished and ready for winter. The settlers had recovered their health and strength, and they had all good things in plenty.

It was time to celebrate the harvest and thank God for the blessings He had bestowed upon them. The Pilgrims sent a message to the Indians, inviting them to join a feast. Then they set about preparing. The men went into the fields and forests to hunt ducks, geese, and turkeys. The women stood beside the fires kneading, slicing, and roasting. The settlers set up long tables outside and placed rough benches beside them.

King Massasoit arrived with ninety of his braves. They brought five deer, their gift to the feast. Then the Pilgrims and Indians shared the bounty of the land. They ate fish and wildfowl and venison. From the bay there were clams, scallops, and oysters. From the forests came nuts and berries, and from the gardens came carrots, turnips, and onions. They feasted on stewed pumpkin, corn cakes, and bowls of chowder.

They celebrated with games as well. The settlers and Indians held shooting contests with both guns and bows. The young men challenged each other in foot races and wrestling matches. The Englishmen did jigs for the Indians, and the Indians in turn showed off their own dances.

For three days the feast continued. The Pilgrims knew well that more days of trial and hardship lay ahead. But for now, they rejoiced together over the gifts they had received. They thanked God for bringing them across the stormy ocean and seeing them through the long, harsh winter. They thanked Him for the bountiful fruits of their labor. They gave thanks for their Indian friends. And they gave thanks for this new land, where they could worship as they pleased.

Every year we remember that long-ago feast called the First Thanksgiving. On the fourth Thursday of each November, we rejoice that friends and loved ones have gathered safely together. We celebrate the fruits of our labor. We recall that throughout our nation's past, our ancestors risked their lives so we might be free. We bow our heads in thanks for all the bounty of this land and for the many blessings we have received.

Father Junipero Serra

In 1769, the king of Spain sent explorers from Mexico to California to begin settling that vast, beautiful land. One of their leaders was a priest named Father Junipero Serra. Often the settlers' efforts seemed doomed, but Father Serra refused to give up. Time and again in American history, such perseverance has made all the difference.

A line of men and beasts crept across the scorched California desert. Spanish soldiers wiped their brows. Mules staggered under bulky loads of supplies. Indian guides trudged wearily. They were looking for a bay called San Diego, but before them the earth lay brown and empty.

In the midst of this party limped a small priest in a gray robe named Padre Junipero Serra. He was born in Spain, but even as a boy he dreamed of exploring the New World. He came not to find gold or jewels but to spread the word of God.

Padre Serra's kind, bright eyes told of a gentle soul. They also spoke of a courage that never failed. "Always go forward and never turn back" was his motto.

The padre was not a young man. He had a sore left leg, which had been bitten by an insect years before and now hurt all the time. He set out bravely, leaning on a stick as he limped along. But before many miles, he was in great pain. The swelling went halfway up his leg until he could no longer walk. The soldiers looked at him and frowned.

"There is no way you can make it. We are sending you back to Mexico."

Padre Serra shook his head.

"I may not make it to San Diego, but it is God's will that I try," he said. "I will not turn back."

That evening he sent for the young man who took care of the mules.

"Son, can you cure my leg?" he asked. The fellow was so surprised he could barely answer.

"But father, I only know how to treat the sores on the mules," he objected.

"Then pretend I am a mule." Padre Serra smiled.

The muleteer gathered the plants he needed, made a medicine, and spread it on the priest's leg. The next morning Padre Serra could walk again. The soldiers stared in amazement.

"This man lets nothing stand in his way," they whispered to each other.

The explorers hauled themselves across the barren land. They saw nothing but rocks, thorns, and sand. They labored up and down steep slopes. They pushed through cactus thickets. Their water supply ran low. Vultures circled overhead, watching and waiting.

The soldiers clutched at their dust-parched throats. They began to argue among themselves and talked of deserting.

"If we don't find water soon, we'll die," they muttered. "Better to turn back now, before it's too late."

"God is watching over us," Padre Serra told them. "We must never give up hope."

Sure enough, soon they came upon a beautiful stream. The desert gave way to more fertile lands, dotted here and there with clumps of trees.

At last they reached a place where the sea curved inland. Looking down on the wide blue bay, they spied two ships that had sailed north from Mexico to meet them. They had reached San Diego. With tears of joy they rushed to join their comrades.

But their happiness soon gave way to grim news. The ships had suffered a long, hard voyage. Many sailors had perished. More lay sick and dying. Their stores of food were running low.

The Spaniards held a council and chose a course of action. One of the ships, the *San Antonio,* would sail back to Mexico for more men and fresh supplies. The rest would try to hold on in California. The soldiers looked at one another uneasily. They knew the odds against them were growing day by day. The future looked dark.

Padre Serra put his fate in the hands of God and went straight to work. The settlers built a few crude huts where the sick could be nursed to health. One of the huts was set aside as a mission church. Padre Serra set up a cross facing the sea. From the branch of a tree he hung a bell. He called the Indians to come and hear about God.

But then followed months of hardship and disappointment. The Indians did not always come when Padre Junipero rang the mission bell. They did not know what to make of these newcomers and their strange ways. One day they attacked the mission. It broke Padre Serra's heart to see God's children fighting.

Sickness spread and more men died. Padre Junipero himself became ill. Almost all the food was gone. The men were always hungry and weak.

Every day the Spaniards looked to sea, hoping the *San Antonio* would return. But day after day there was no sign of aid. No word came from Mexico—only silence.

It seemed madness to stay any longer, and so a decision was made—they would pack up and go home. But Padre Serra begged his comrades to wait a while longer.

"In nine days it will be the Feast of Saint Joseph," he said. "Wait until then. If the *San Antonio* has not arrived, I, too, will admit defeat."

The padre's faith touched every heart. It was agreed to hang on a bit longer. Each day Padre Serra prayed, but each day the ocean lay empty. St. Joseph's Day arrived. The soldiers packed and prepared to go.

The afternoon shadows lengthened. The sun sank toward the sea.

"Have hope," Padre Serra whispered. "The day is not yet over."

The soldiers smiled at each other sadly. This man refused to give up!

Then someone pointed toward the water. A speck appeared on the horizon. The men held their breaths and watched.

"A sail! A sail!" The cry ran through the camp. It was the *San Antonio*, bringing men and food and medicine.

Was it a miracle? Those who watched Padre Serra fall to his knees and give thanks thought surely the good man's prayers had been answered.

The San Diego mission grew and flourished. It was only the first. Padre Serra and his comrades proceeded to found a string of missions along the California coast. At each one they hung a bell to chime the hour and summon all to prayer.

Some of the old missions still stand. When Americans hear the ringing of their bells, they remember the gentle little priest who limped hundreds of miles up and down California, telling of God and cheering others with these words: "Always go forward and never turn back."

The Bravery of
Abigail Adams

The Revolutionary War years were a terrible and dangerous time. Many patriots had to flee their homes, and many lost everything they owned. Others suffered one of life's hardest challenges—they were torn from their loved ones. Abigail and John Adams spent many years apart during the period of our nation's founding, but their love for America and each other pulled them through.

The year was 1775, and sparks of rebellion whirled through the air. The American colonists were talking about freedom from England. British Redcoats swarmed through the streets of Boston. Patriots held secret meetings while men such as Paul Revere jumped on their horses and galloped from town to town, carrying news and warnings. Minutemen—farmers and tradesmen ready to fight on a moment's notice—shouldered their muskets and marched toward Boston. Everyone wondered if America and Britain were on the road to war.

In the village of Braintree, near Boston, Abigail Adams struggled amid the confusion and alarm. Her husband, John, was far away in Philadelphia at a meeting of the Continental Congress. There, leaders such as George Washington, Thomas Jefferson, and Benjamin Franklin were gathering to plot America's future. With John in Philadelphia, it was up to Abigail to care for the children and manage the farm alone.

There was much to do. The cows must be milked, the orchards tended, the accounts balanced. There were shirts to be sewn and pots to stir in the big kitchen fireplace. Many things were in short supply—sugar, pepper, pins—so Abigail did without them. Since the schools were closed because of the danger, the children were taught at home.

Minutemen, hungry and thirsty, tramped past the door, and Abigail gave them food and drink. Patriot families, fleeing Boston, poured into the countryside. Abigail spread blankets on the floor and gave shelter to as many as she could.

Abigail loved her husband and wanted him at her side in these unnerving times. But she also knew that America needed him for a while.

Almost every day she wrote to John, telling him about the children and the farm. She reported on the troubles in Boston and sent him her love and prayers.

"Good night. With thoughts of thee I close my eyes. Angels guard and protect thee."

All around her, Abigail could see and hear signs of danger. The countryside was filled with the sounds of men marching, drums beating, church bells ringing in alarm. Neighbors took sides against one another. Rumors spread like wildfire. There was news of bloodshed at Lexington and Concord, talk of fresh British troops sailing into Boston, warnings that the Redcoats were marching this way to arrest rebellious Patriots.

"In case of real danger," John wrote, "fly to the woods with our children."

Abigail responded bravely.

"Courage I know we have in abundance, conduct I hope we shall not want," she wrote, "but gunpowder—where shall we get a sufficient supply?"

Early one morning, before the sun rose, Abigail woke to a distant rumble. For a moment she lay still, listening for what she thought must be thunder. The deep booming came again, rolling across the hills from Boston. She leaped out of bed and dressed hastily by candlelight.

The noise woke her young son, Johnny, too. Taking him by the hand, Abigail climbed through orchards to the top of a nearby hill. They held their breaths and peered through the graying dawn.

Off toward Boston, smoke hung on the horizon. A far-away fiery glow filled the hazy air. Distant rockets burst in the sky and cannon blasts shattered the early morning stillness.

"What is it, Mother?" Johnny asked.

Abigail felt his eyes upon her, wide and uncertain, and she shuddered, for she knew it was the start of a long and terrible struggle for liberty—and that America's fate now hung in the balance.

Several days later in far-off Philadelphia, a gloomy John Adams sat in his boardinghouse room, his spirits sinking like a stone. He had just received a letter from Abigail telling of a terrible battle at Bunker Hill. Many brave men had fallen on both sides.

John was sick with worry about his family. Were they safe? Did they have enough food to eat? Where would they go if the Redcoats ran them out of their home?

He despaired at the slow work of the Continental Congress. There was so much squabbling among its members. How were the colonies to govern themselves? How could the rag-tag Patriot army stand up to the king's soldiers? Where would George Washington find enough men and muskets to fight?

Tired and lonely, John rose and paced the hot room. A frown creased his forehead. Perhaps the fight for liberty was a hopeless cause. Then his eyes fell on a few words in Abigail's letter.

"The race is not to the swift, nor the battle to the strong, but the God of Israel is he that giveth strength and power unto his people. Trust in him at all times. . . ."

Tears of love and pride sprang to his eyes. He thought of his wife's courage and faith. Even as danger swirled all around her, she somehow carried on with the task of counseling her husband, protecting her family, and aiding the Patriot cause.

The clouds of doubt parted. With such bravery and devotion, nothing was impossible. John Adams knew the colonies could win their freedom. With fresh strength he picked up his pen and went back to the work of founding a new and great nation.

"Yankee Doodle"

The Spirit of '76 echoes in this song. British troops originally sang it to make fun of the shabby Colonial army, but the hard-fighting Americans liked the tune so much, they made it their own during the Revolutionary War. "Yankee" was a nickname for New Englanders, "doodle" meant a foolish fellow, and "macaroni" was slang for a dandy who liked to dress in style.

Yankee Doodle went to town,
A-ridin' on a pony,
Stuck a feather in his hat
And called it macaroni.

Chorus:
Yankee Doodle, keep it up,
Yankee Doodle Dandy,
Mind the music and the step
And with the girls be handy.

Father and I went down to camp
Along with Captain Gooding,
And there we saw the men and boys
As thick as hasty pudding.

Yankee · Doodle · went · to · town ·

And there was Captain Washington
Upon a slapping stallion,
A-giving orders to his men,
I guess there were a million.

And there I saw a wooden drum
With heads made out of leather,
They knocked upon it with some sticks
To call the folks together.

And then they'd fife away like fun
And play on cornstalk fiddles,
And some had ribbons red as blood
All bound around their middles.

Uncle Sam came there to change
Some pancakes and some onions
For 'lasses cakes to carry home
To give his wife and young ones.

But I can't tell you half I saw,
They kept up such a smother,
So I took my hat off, made a bow,
And scampered home to mother.

A·ridin'·on·a·pony

Westward with
Lewis and Clark

*The very first journey across our country and back took more than two years!
Travel is faster these days, but blazing new trails is still the American way.*

Two hundred years ago, most of this country was a wild, unexplored land that stretched toward the setting sun. Great rivers flowed out of the western frontiers, but where did they come from? There were rumors of rugged mountains, but how high did they reach? Somewhere beyond the mountains lay the Pacific Ocean. How far away was the sea? No one knew.

One morning in 1804, a clumsy-looking barge with a big square sail pushed up the wide Missouri River. Behind it came two long sturdy canoes called pirogues. All three boats were loaded with men and supplies. On the deck of the barge, two men stood talking. Their names were Captain Meriwether Lewis and Captain William Clark. They were setting out to do what no one had ever done before—travel across America to the great Pacific Ocean.

Washington, D.C.

St. Louis

UNITED
STATES

President Thomas Jefferson was sending this party to explore the boundless frontier. He wanted Lewis and Clark to find a path that would lead across the country. So this brave group of adventurers said goodbye to their friends and loved ones and started west into uncharted lands.

Progress up the Missouri River was hard and slow. Sometimes the explorers pushed the barge upstream with long poles. Sometimes they trudged along the riverbanks, towing the boat with a long rope. Captain Lewis and Captain Clark took turns scouting the land, collecting leaves, flowers, rocks, and even dinosaur bones to send back to Thomas Jefferson. They drew maps of their route so that others could someday follow.

The prairies stretched as far as the eye could see. The land teemed with deer, turkeys, and geese, which the explorers hunted for dinner. At night, the sky filled with blazing stars. Wolves howled. Bears rustled in the bushes. Sometimes, when the men rose in the gray dawn, they shook rattlesnakes from their blankets.

Soon they reached Indian territory, where tribes such as the Otoes, the Omahas, and the Sioux lived. Captain Lewis and Captain Clark held councils with the Indians. The proud chiefs came dressed in their finery—their skin painted yellow and red and green, their hair decorated with feathers and porcupine quills, their throats gleaming with bear-claw necklaces. Sometimes the Indians welcomed these newcomers as friends. Some tribes, however, feared that these strangers came to rob them of their lands. Always Lewis and Clark kept their eyes open and their guns within reach, ready for any surprise.

On the explorers pushed. Great plains spread before them, covered with herds of buffalo, elk, and antelope. Prairie dogs scampered into their holes. Beavers splashed by the river's shores. The land's size and bounty seemed to go on forever.

But now cold weather approached. Ice began to float down the river and the northern lights danced overhead at night. The tired explorers halted to build a winter camp. They crawled under buffalo blankets and snored while the blizzards piled snowdrifts all around their log cabins.

One day a French trader named Charbonneau arrived at the little outpost. Lewis and Clark decided to make him a part of their expedition since he spoke the Indians' language. With him came his young Shoshoni wife, Sacagawea, a name that meant "bird woman." That winter Sacagawea gave birth to a son, Jean Baptiste.

At last the snows melted and it was time to start out again. The big barge was loaded with everything the explorers had gathered so far—Indian clothes, animal skins, plants, insects, even live birds and a prairie dog— and sent back downstream to President Jefferson. The explorers, meanwhile, headed farther west. With the two pirogues and six new canoes they pushed upstream, into the unknown.

Sacagawea pushed steadily forward, too, carrying little Baptiste on a papoose board. It did not take her long to show her courage and quick thinking. One day a squall overturned one of the pirogues. The boat filled with water. Clothing, equipment, medicine, and all sorts of valuable instruments floated away. With her infant strapped to her back, Sacagawea plucked the supplies from the icy river. If they had been lost, the explorers might have been forced to turn back.

The land began to grow steep with hills. The men hauled the boats with tow ropes, wading waist-deep in the cold, swift water. High cliffs loomed over the river, worn into a thousand strange shapes like castles, columns, and towers.

They came to a place where the river forked into two large streams. Which way led to the mountains? The captains looked at the streams. In one, the water was muddy, but the other flowed clear over a bed of stones, like water coming out of highlands. They decided to follow this branch.

How would they know if they had chosen the right path? The Indians had said they would find a mighty waterfall on the river that led to the mountains. Tramping onward, the explorers came to a roaring wall of water. They were on the right track. They had reached the Great Falls of the Missouri.

The waterfalls were magnificent, but they were also a problem. The boats and everything else would have to be carried around them. The men cut down a cottonwood tree and made wagons to haul their supplies. Then the back-breaking work began. They pushed and pulled, dragging their cargo across the savage land. They caught at stones and bushes to haul the carts up the slopes. The prickly-pear cactus spines cut through their moccasins. Mosquitoes swarmed in the broiling heat. It took nearly a month to portage around the falls.

But now an even greater obstacle stood in their way—the snow-capped Rocky Mountains, vaulting toward the sky. Somehow they must get over these peaks.

Sacagawea pointed out landmarks she once knew as a child. Here, years ago, she had lived with her Shoshoni people. One day, without warning, an enemy tribe had swept into their valley. The warriors had seized little Sacagawea and carried her far away. Now, at last, she was returning home.

Soon the explorers found the Shoshoni and sat down to talk with Cameahwait, their chief. Sacagawea spoke as Lewis and Clark's interpreter. Suddenly, with a cry of delight, she jumped up and threw her arms around Cameahwait. She had discovered that he was her own brother!

Sacagawea told her people about Lewis and Clark's long journey. Chief Cameahwait agreed to sell them horses for the trip across the mountains. Two Indian guides would go along to show them the way. But they must hurry. Another winter would soon be upon them.

The explorers set out again. The hillsides were so steep that the horses kept slipping and falling. The brush was tangled and the men had to hack a trail as they pushed along. Rain, sleet, and snow fell. The food supply gave out, and the weary explorers began to go hungry. On and on they plunged through the snowdrifts, wondering if their journey would come to an awful end here in these high, craggy mountains. But at last they stumbled down onto a plain where some Indians gave them food.

With the mountains behind them, Captain Clark set the men about the task of making dugout canoes. Now the explorers would be able to ride the rivers to the ocean. Their goal was within reach.

Downstream they dashed on the great Columbia River. The boiling waters rushed through canyons and foamed over jagged boulders. More than once the boats turned over or crashed against hidden rocks. But at last the river widened and its current slowed. A white fog hung over its surface, and its waters began to move with the ebb and flow of the sea.

One morning the fog lifted. The weary voyagers stared ahead, barely able to believe their eyes. An endless expanse of water lay before them. They had reached the Pacific Ocean.

They had done it, crossing the vast stretches of land no one had dared to cross before. When Lewis and Clark found their way home again, more than two years after their departure, they brought word of a country richer and wider than anyone had dreamed. Towering mountains, endless plains, and fertile valleys were waiting. Now the path was open for the pioneers who would settle the nation from sea to sea. This brave group of men, and this one valiant Indian woman who traveled across a continent with her child on her back, had shown the way. They had shown just how big and great America was.

Paul Bunyan

Paul Bunyan reminds us that in America the sky—and our imaginations—is the limit. This is a land of big ideas, boundless energy, and mighty deeds.

Without a doubt, Paul Bunyan was the biggest, strongest, greatest lumberjack in history. No one knows for certain exactly how tall ol' Paul stood. But we do know that each morning he combed his big black beard with a pine tree to turn out any bobcats that had bedded down in his whiskers. When he swung his giant ax, he felled thirty trees at once and spawned tornadoes from Illinois to Oklahoma.

Most folks say Paul was born in Maine. (Some say he was born in five or six states all at once, he was so big.) He caused a lot of trouble as a baby, since every time he kicked or crawled around, he knocked down a few miles of fences, barns, and orchards. After a while the neighbors started complaining, so his parents built him a giant cradle and anchored it in the Atlantic Ocean. But every time he rocked in his cradle, the waves swamped two or three coastal towns. Once he fell overboard and caused a tidal wave. So his parents had to bring him back to port.

After that Mr. and Mrs. Bunyan decided to move to the wilderness, where Paul got plenty of practice knocking down trees as he was growing up. That's where he got the idea to invent logging. At first, he worked all by himself. But as word of his mighty feats spread and people heard about how he was clearing the wilderness to build the country, men started flocking from all over the world to lend a hand.

Before you knew it, Paul had hundreds of lumbermen working for him. He and his crew were always one step ahead of civilization, clearing the way for settlers and cutting the wood to build homes, churches, and schoolhouses. Before long, they'd cleared most of the forests in the East, and that part of the country was filling up with people. So Paul and his crew headed west to Wisconsin, where they set up camp.

Of course, cutting down trees works up an appetite, so the first thing Paul had to do was build a great big camp kitchen. The cookhouse was three miles long. The stove covered an acre of ground. It took a whole forest of firewood just to heat it up at sunrise. Seven lumbermen greased the griddle every morning by strapping slabs of bacon to their feet and skating across the sizzling surface.

Flapjacks, of course, are what lumbermen like best, so that's what Paul's cook, Sourdough Sam, made for breakfast. He made big flapjacks for the men and giant ones for Paul himself. As fast as he could cook them, three assistant chefs scooped them off the stove top with shovels and pitched them onto horse-drawn wagons for a mad dash to the mess hall. Wagons carrying the syrup sped right behind. (Paul dug the St. Lawrence River so that big barges of New England maple syrup could be floated to his camp.)

Paul kept the whole camp—kitchen, mess hall, bunk-houses and all—on a giant sled. When all the timber in a region was cut, he hitched Babe the Big Blue Ox to the sled and pulled the camp off to a new frontier. As Paul moved on, the farms and villages moved in behind him.

Paul had found Babe buried in a snowdrift during the Winter of the Blue Snow. (After all the snow had melted, Paul and his bookkeeper, Johnny Inkslinger, turned it into ink, so folks could write tales like the one you're reading now.) Babe was just a calf when Paul found him, but he was already pretty large, and he just kept growing and growing. He grew two feet every time Paul looked at him.

No one knows for sure exactly how big Babe grew to be, but old lumbermen swear he measured forty-seven ax handles between the eyes, and was heavier than the combined weight of all the fish that ever got away. Every time Babe needed to be shod, they had to dig a brand new Minnesota iron mine. Paul's blacksmith, Big Swede Ole, sank knee-deep in solid rock with every step when he carried Babe's shoes.

Of course, feeding Babe was a problem. He ate fifty bales of hay for a snack, and then it took six men to brush his teeth. Once his water trough sprang a leak, which is what started the Mississippi River flowing. After that, Paul dug the Great Lakes so Babe would have a watering hole.

Babe could pull just about anything you could hitch a chain to. Take, for example, the time he pulled the River That Ran Sideways into shape. The river was only twenty

miles long from north to south, but it had so many loops and bends and doubled back on itself so many times that it ran 212 miles from east to west. It took nearly two years to float logs downstream. That didn't suit Paul at all. Finally he spiked a chain to each bank, hitched Babe to the river, and yelled for him to pull. The big ox hunched his shoulders and gave a mighty yank. All the kinks came out, and after that the river was straight as a shotgun barrel.

Babe was a big help when the Winter of the Deep Snow came along, too. That was the winter it got so cold, the smoke coming out of the bunkhouse chimney froze in a column two miles high. Every morning one of the lumbermen had to climb up on the roof and chop it down. The boiling coffee froze so fast the ice got too hot to handle. It snowed and snowed and snowed till the tops of the trees got buried, and Paul's men couldn't find them to cut them down.

Finally Paul got an idea. He asked Ole the blacksmith to make a pair of giant, green-tinted glasses for Babe and turned him out to graze in the snowdrifts. When the Big Blue Ox saw the world colored green, he thought the hills were covered with clover and ate all the snow for lunch.

When Paul got through logging in Michigan, Minnesota, and thereabouts, he moved down the center of the country, through places like Nebraska and Kansas. He logged an awful lot of trees there and, while he was at it, cut down the hills for good measure. He leveled them flat as flapjacks so we'd have the Great Plains, and the farmers could plant miles of wheat for the growing nation.

Next, Paul and his crew logged the Southwest desert. That was the summer Babe got so thirsty, he drank all the water out of the Long Gone River and all the other rivers for miles and miles around. There's never been much water in the desert since then.

After he cleared the desert, Paul headed for the great Northwest, where he dug the Columbia River Gorge so that he could float his logs to the Pacific Ocean. But after a while even that corner of the country started filling up with people, making it hard for Paul to log on the kind of grand scale that suited him.

Some say he decided to hang up his ax. But most folks hold that Paul headed up to Alaska, where there's lots of untouched, wide open space left, and real frontier work to be done. There he strides across the mountains to log the frozen forests with Babe and treks up to the North Pole when he feels like stretching his legs a bit. Sometimes, just for fun, he breaks off huge hunks of ice and tosses them into the ocean for Babe to fetch, which is why the ships up there always have to be on the lookout for icebergs.

Wherever he is, you can be sure Paul is still busy. When you hear distant thunder rumbling, you know that's just the sound of him felling big trees, or moving mountains, or maybe laughing his deep, long laugh after a good day's labor. Wherever he is, you can bet your last dollar he's working hard, helping the country grow bigger and stronger.

The Story of "The Star Spangled Banner"

⁓ ADAPTED FROM EVA MARCH TAPPAN

The story behind our national anthem is a story of perseverance in defense of liberty. The battle at Fort McHenry that inspired the song took place during the War of 1812. In 1931, Congress chose "The Star Spangled Banner" as our national anthem.

The year 1814 found the people of Maryland in trouble. America was again at war with Great Britain, and a British fleet had sailed into the Chesapeake Bay. All along the shores, people fired alarms and lit signal fires to let their neighbors know danger was near. The ships sailed up the bay toward Baltimore. The bustling port was a rich prize. To take it, however, the British fleet would have to get past Fort McHenry, which guarded Baltimore's harbor.

As the warships crept upstream toward the fort, the crews could see a giant flag with fifteen white stars and fifteen red and white stripes flapping above the ramparts. It was the work of Baltimore flag-maker Mary Young Pickersgill and her thirteen-year-old daughter, Caroline. Their own house had not been large enough for the job of stitching together the enormous banner, so they had done some of the sewing in a nearby brewery where they could spread it across the wide floor. Now it flew as the proud symbol of an upstart country that was about to take on the most powerful nation in the world.

On the morning of September 13, the big British guns took aim at the flag and let loose a terrible fire. They shot huge bombshells that often blew up in midair. The attack lasted all day. When dark fell, the fleet used signal rockets, which traced fiery arcs across the night sky. It was a spectacular sight.

"If Fort McHenry can stand, the city is safe," Francis Scott Key muttered to himself. He stared anxiously through the smoke to see if the flag was still flying.

The young Washington lawyer was watching the battle from a little American vessel floating with the British ships. He had sailed out to the British fleet under a flag of truce before the fighting began. A friend had been seized prisoner by the British, and Key went to ask for his release. The British commander agreed, but he would not let Key return to Baltimore with any information he might have picked up. "Until the battle is over, you and your boat stay here," he ordered.

Key had no choice but to wait it out, pacing the deck and hoping the fort could hold out. The firing went on and on. As long as the daylight lasted, he could catch glimpses of the Stars and Stripes through the clouds of smoke. When night came, he could still see the banner now and then by the blaze of the cannon.

Finally, toward daybreak, the firing stopped. Key strained to see if the flag was still flying. "Could the fort have held out?" he wondered.

The faint gray of dawn crept into the sky. He could see that some flag was flying—but was it American or British? Who held Fort McHenry?

More and more eagerly he gazed. It grew lighter. A sudden breath of wind caught the banner and it floated out on

the breeze. This was no English flag; it was Mary Pickersgill's Stars and Stripes, still waving through the smoke and mist! Fort McHenry had stood, and the city was safe!

Overcome with joy, Key snatched an old letter from his pocket. Still watching the flag, he began scribbling a few lines on its back.

The British departed and the little American boat sailed back to the city. Key gave a copy of the poem he had just written to his brother-in-law, who had helped defend the fort. His brother-in-law sent it to a printer and had it struck off on some handbills. Before the ink was dry, the printer snatched one up and hurried to a tavern where many patriots were assembling.

"Listen to this!" he cried, and he read the verse to the crowd.

"Sing it! Sing it!" the whole company cried. Someone mounted a chair and sang the poem to an old tune. The song caught on at once. Halls, theaters, and houses soon rang with its strains as the British fleet disappeared over the horizon.

The years passed, and Francis Scott Key's words found a place in his fellow citizens' hearts. They became the anthem of a nation that stands always for freedom, just as the Stars and Stripes stood through that perilous fight so long ago.

"The Star Spangled Banner"

O say, can you see by the dawn's early light,
What so proudly we hailed at the twilight's last gleaming,
Whose broad stripes and bright stars, through the perilous fight
O'er the ramparts we watch'd were so gallantly streaming?
And the rockets' red glare, the bombs bursting in air,
Gave proof through the night that our flag was still there.
O say, does that Star Spangled Banner yet wave
O'er the land of the free and the home of the brave?

Johnny Appleseed

John Chapman's simple, giving life made him a legend in his own day. When news of his death in 1845 reached Washington, Sam Houston stood up in Congress and said: "Farewell, dear old eccentric heart. Your labor has been a labor of love, and generations yet unborn will rise up and call you blessed." This humble pioneer's spirit lives on in the lore of Johnny Appleseed.

There's a wanderer, they say, in the Ohio Valley. He comes by at apple blossom time. Get out of bed early, just as the sun rises, and you might see smoke hanging over the orchard as his breakfast fire dies low. Wait a while longer and a breeze comes rustling through the trees. The old farmers wink and smile.

"Here he comes, waking the blossoms to a new spring," they say. "That's Johnny Appleseed passing by."

John Chapman was his real name. Folks in Pittsburgh say he had a big flowering orchard there, way back when the country was new. Day after day he sat on his fence and watched covered wagons rolling by, full of pioneer families, headed west.

"Rough lives await them, full of hardship and toil," he thought. "What can I do to help?"

He watched the wagons go rumbling by and an idea took root in his mind. It grew and grew until it turned into a plan. So he filled a bag with apple seeds and slung it over his shoulder. Then he wandered away.

John walked through woods filled with oaks and hickories. He crossed fields where tall grasses waved in the wind.

Every once in a while, beside a stream or in a clearing, he would pause and untie his bag. With a pointed stick he dug holes, then stooped and planted some seeds. He covered them well, knowing they would grow in the sunshine and rain.

When the wagons came rolling west, the seedlings were green and strong. He dug them up carefully and gave them to pioneer families.

"Set them in the earth, and someday you'll harvest nature's jewels!" he told them. "Apples! Apple butter! Apple sauce! Apple cider! Jelly and pie!"

The settlers smiled and took the seedlings gladly. They planted orchards beside their new homes.

People began to call him Johnny Appleseed.

On he went. When his shoes wore out, he walked in his bare feet. Whenever he tore a hole in his shirt, he just took his needle and thread and sewed on a patch. For a hat he wore the old tin pot he used to cook his dinner.

"This is all I need," he would say. "God has made me rich, for I'm helping my fellow man."

Far and wide he traveled, across hills and valleys, through summer storms and winter snow. When night fell, he stretched out on a hillside. A mound of moss was his pillow, the starry sky his roof. When morning broke he would rise and walk on.

His orchards spread across the frontier, and so did Johnny Appleseed's fame.

Sometimes an Indian came striding along and walked with him through the wilds. But more often than not, he walked alone. Then, they say, the birds perched on his shoulder and deer ate from his hand. Sometimes he would pause and play with bear cubs while the mother bear looked on.

When a log cabin came into view, Johnny Appleseed was always welcome to rest his weary feet. Around the big fireplace the family would gather. The children lay on the floor, and Johnny would pull his Bible from his coffee sack shirt.

"Here's news straight from Heaven," he'd say. He would read of Noah's ark or the Sermon on the Mount.

His voice was so gentle and his smile so kind, they always asked him to stay awhile. He'd shake his head. "I've got work to do. Got to be on my way."

Ohio filled up with fences and barns and orchards.

"Time to be moving on," Johnny said. He headed west, planting seeds for the country as it moved west, too.

Some say he came to rest in Indiana, beneath the bough of an apple tree. Others say he just kept walking. Who knows how far he got? All across America—in the hills of Tennessee, the plains of Nebraska, the slopes of the Rockies, the wide valleys of California—people point to orchards and say: "Johnny Appleseed planted these trees."

Maybe he's been your way, too.

Abe Lincoln's School Days

"My best friend is the man who will lend me a book," young Abraham Lincoln used to say. The life of this backwoods boy still inspires our American faith that with enough hard work and study, any one of us can rise to the top.

Just about everyone who knew young Abe Lincoln remembered two things about him—his legs were forever getting longer, so his buckskin britches were always too short, and he always had a book in his hands.

Books weren't as plentiful as wildcats in the parts of Kentucky and Indiana where Abe grew up. But he read every one he could find. All the money he saved went to buy books, and he borrowed them from friends whenever he could. He once walked twenty miles just to borrow a book he wanted to read.

Abe walked to school, too, trudging hand-in-hand with his sister, Sarah, through forests where deer bounded, bears rustled, and squirrels chattered high overhead. The little log schoolhouse had just one room. The floor was dirt and the students sat on split-log benches. They learned their lessons by reciting them out loud, all at once. Some said their A-B-Cs, while others said their 1-2-3s. It was called a blab school because of the jumble of noise.

Abe learned to read, write, add, and subtract. The teacher taught manners, too, like how to say "Howdy do?" when you opened a door and walked into a room.

But frontier life was hard and left almost no time for sitting in class. There were always fields to be plowed, seeds to be planted, and rails to be split for fences. Abe used to joke that he went to school "by littles." He went a little bit when he was seven and a little bit more when he was eleven. He went a little when he was thirteen and went back a little while longer when he was fifteen. All together, he spent less than a year in school.

But what he tasted of books in class made him hunger for more. He would stuff a book into his shirt and go off to plow or hoe. When lunchtime came, he would sit in the shade of a tree and read. When he came home in the evening, he would go to the cupboard, snatch a piece of cornbread, take down a book, and read until his candle went out.

When Abe came across a passage that struck him, he copied it down so he could read it over and over again until he knew it by heart. If he didn't have paper, he wrote on a board, or a fence rail, or even the floor.

He did his arithmetic at night, too. He sat by the chimney and wrote numbers with charcoal on a wooden fire shovel, adding and subtracting by the light of the fire. When the shovel was covered with numbers, he shaved them off with a knife and started over.

Our future president liked to lie on his stomach beside the fire and read to sister Sarah. He read *Aesop's Fables*, *Pilgrim's Progress*, *Robinson Crusoe*, and *The Arabian Nights*. When he got a little older, he read the Declaration of Independence, and the U.S. Constitution. He wondered at the rich, mysterious phrases he found in the family Bible, too.

Once he borrowed a book about George Washington from a neighboring farmer. He read until he went to bed, then he put it on a little shelf where he thought it would be safe. But that night it stormed. The rain found its way into a crack between two logs in the wall and soaked the book through and through. It was almost ruined.

Abe felt very uneasy for the book was precious in his eyes, as well as in the eyes of its owner. He took the stained volume and set out for his neighbor's house.

"Well, Abe, what brings you here so early?" asked Mr. Crawford.

"I've got bad news," said a long-faced Abe.

"Bad news! What is it?"

"You know the book you lent me, *The Life of Washington*?"

"Yes, yes."

"Well, the rain spoiled it last night." He showed the book, wet to a pulp inside, and honestly explained how it happened.

"That's too bad, Abe," said his neighbor, stroking his chin.

"I don't have any money, Mr. Crawford," the young man said. "But I can work. I'll work on your farm till I've paid for the book."

Abe worked three days in his neighbor's cornfield until he'd made up for the loss.

"You've done a good job," Mr. Crawford said. "I guess you can keep the book."

Abe walked home that night with the book under his arm and a lesson lodged in his heart. He was sorry about what had happened but proud to have made amends and happy to have the book for his own, since George Washington was one of his heroes.

So he went on working and reading and growing. By small degrees he gained deep understanding. The boy who went to a one-room schoolhouse "by littles," who wrote on boards when he had no paper, who walked miles through the woods just to borrow a book, slowly became one of our country's wisest and greatest men.

"The Erie Canal"

Completed in 1825, before the age of the railroads, the Erie Canal was the nation's great water highway, connecting the Hudson River and Great Lakes. Boatmen sang this song as their plodding mules pulled barges between Albany and Buffalo, New York. Riders on canal boats might get a bump on the head if they failed to heed the mule driver's warning: "Low bridge, everybody down!"

I've got a mule, her name is Sal,
Fifteen miles on the Erie Canal.
She's a good old worker and a good old pal,
Fifteen miles on the Erie Canal.
We've hauled some barges in our day,
Filled with lumber, coal and hay,
And every inch of the way we know,
From Albany to Buffalo.

Chorus:
Low bridge, everybody down!
Low bridge, for we're going through a town!
And you'll always know your neighbor,
You'll always know your pal,
If you ever navigated on the Erie Canal.

We better get along on our way, old gal,
Fifteen miles on the Erie Canal.
'Cause you bet your life I'd never part with Sal,
Fifteen miles on the Erie Canal.
Git up there, mule, here comes a lock,
We'll make Rome 'bout six o'clock.
One more trip and back we'll go
Right back home to Buffalo.

Remember the Alamo!

Building this country took grit—sometimes the great courage to stand fast in the line of fire even when all hope was gone.

An alarm spread across Texas in early 1836. A great Mexican army led by General Santa Anna was marching from the south. In a few short days it would cross the Rio Grande River. Anyone who stood in its way would surely be destroyed.

In those times, Texas was part of Mexico. Santa Anna had seized power, made himself dictator, and demanded that all citizens submit to his rule. But the people of Texas refused. They made up their minds to fight for freedom.

The Texans hurried to arm themselves. Some gathered at an old mission once built by Spanish friars, a place called the Alamo. Here they would make their stand.

The Alamo was not much of a fortress. It was little more than a big stone building, a ruined chapel, and a large yard surrounded by a high wall. The men inside knew they would be outnumbered. But they would rather face a whole army than submit to Santa Anna's rule.

The defenders came from far and wide. There was young William Travis from South Carolina, the commander of the Alamo. There was Jim Bowie, who grew up among the blackwater swamps and tangled bayous of Louisiana. Bowie was famous for riding alligators and lassoing wild cattle, and even more famous for the way he handled his knife. Folks said that knife could tickle a fellow's ribs a long time without making him laugh.

Also at the Alamo was the great teller of tales and killer of bears Davy Crockett from Tennessee, in his coonskin cap and buckskin coat. Davy was already a legend. People said he could whip his weight in wildcats and grin a raccoon right out of a tree. With his long rifle, Betsy, he could shoot the wick out from under a candle flame.

Most of the men inside the Alamo were not famous, though. Most were not soldiers. They were ordinary men who had grown tough in lives of danger and hardship, men who had tamed the wilderness. They were fewer than 200 in number, but they had a love of liberty and knew how to stand up for themselves.

At last the Mexican army arrived. The church bells in town announced their presence. Santa Anna ordered a red flag raised atop the belfry. It meant: "Surrender or die. We will take no prisoners."

The Texans answered with a cannon shot. They would never give up.

Colonel Travis knew that to have a chance, he needed more men. He sent messengers bearing appeals for aid. "Our flag still waves proudly from the walls," he wrote. "I call on you in the name of liberty, of patriotism, and everything dear to the American character, to come to our aid with all dispatch. . . . If this call is neglected, I am determined to sustain myself as long as possible and die like a soldier who never forgets what is due to his own honor and that of his country. *Victory or death.*"

The messengers departed and the men inside the Alamo waited. The Mexican army spread out around the fort and began to tighten its grip. Their cannon boomed, testing the strength of the old stone walls. In the lulls between the thundering fire, a strange sound floated on the smoke-filled air. It was music. Davy Crockett was fiddling inside the walls, raising the spirits of his comrades.

Days passed, and help finally came when thirty-two men slipped through the enemy lines and joined the force inside the Alamo. But that was all. The Texans now numbered 184 fighting men. Meanwhile, the Mexican army had been growing, too, swelling to 6,000 strong.

William Travis called his men together. He told them there would be no one else coming. If anyone wanted to try to escape, he would not hold him back. Now was the time to choose. He drew his sword and scratched a long line in the dust. All who wished to remain should step over the line.

They all crossed over, except one man. All but one elected to stand and fight.

The attack came early the next morning, before the sun rose. The cold, dark stillness was splintered by the blare of bugles, the crack of musket fire, and shouts of charging soldiers. They came from all four sides.

The Texas riflemen stood coolly atop the walls. Their deadly aim did its work. The first assault of the Mexican army wavered, broke, and fell back. The men inside the Alamo cheered.

The brave Mexicans rushed forward in a second charge. Once more the Texans drove them away.

But now came a third wave, and this time the Texans could not hold them back. The Mexican soldiers reached the fort, threw up their scaling ladders, and swarmed over the walls. In a few moments the battle was over. Not one of the Alamo's defenders was left alive. Colonel Travis, Jim Bowie, the great Davy Crockett—all were gone.

Santa Anna had taken the Alamo, but at a cost of hundreds of troops and a great delay. The stand-off at the Alamo gave other Texans time to rally their defenses. And it made them determined to fight even harder. "Remember the Alamo!" became the battle cry of the Texas army that soon met and broke Santa Anna's force.

The fight for independence was over. The dictator was defeated and Texans were free. Ten years later, in 1846, Texas became part of the United States.

To this day, we remember the story of the small band that stood unflinching against overwhelming odds, even to the last man. We honor their courage and devotion to liberty. And we recall that many brave Americans have laid down their lives in defense of freedom, whenever we hear the battle cry:

Remember the Alamo!

"I Hear America Singing"

~ WALT WHITMAN

These lines are from Walt Whitman's book Leaves of Grass, *first published in 1855. Whitman was the poet of the common man. To him, the songs people sang as they toiled were among the most beautiful sounds on earth. The "varied carols" of Americans working hard still ring today, louder and stronger than ever.*

I hear America singing, the varied carols I hear.
Those of the mechanics, each one singing his as it should be,
    blithe and strong,
The carpenter singing his as he measures his plank or beam,
The mason singing his as he makes ready for work, or
    leaves off work,
The boatman singing what belongs to him in his boat,
    the deckhand singing on the steamboat deck,
The shoemaker singing as he sits on his bench, the hatter
    singing as he stands,
The woodcutter's song, the ploughboy's on his way in the
    morning, or at the noon intermission, or at sundown,
The delicious singing of the mother, or of the young wife
    at work, or of the girl sewing or washing
Each singing what belongs to him or her and to none else,
The day what belongs to the day—at night the part of
    young fellows, robust, friendly,
Singing with open mouths their strong melodious songs.

The Tale of "Swing Low, Sweet Chariot"

Spirituals composed by unknown slaves rank among America's most beautiful music. As this story tells, it is wonderfully fitting that an ex-slave named Ella Sheppard grew up to help introduce "Swing Low, Sweet Chariot" and other spirituals to the world.

Sarah Hannah Sheppard stood beside the Cumberland River in Tennessee. In her arms she clutched her young child. Tears slid down her cheeks and her heart choked with grief. Sarah was a slave, and the day was fast coming when she would be sent away to a Mississippi plantation. Her mistress would not let her take the little girl with her.

She stared into the dark water and hugged Ella tighter. She could not bear the thought of losing her child. Better to jump into the swift, deep current and let the river carry them both away forever.

As she stumbled along the bank, an old woman rounded a curve in the road. She saw what Sarah was about to do and stretched out her hand.

"Don't you do it, honey," she called. "Wait a while and trust in the Lord. Let His sweet chariot swing low."

Sarah stopped in surprise. The old woman came closer. She peered into little Ella's face as if her aged eyes could see a long way.

"There is great work for this child to do here on earth," she said softly. "She's going to stand before kings and queens. So don't you do it, honey. Just you wait. The Lord's going to carry the both of you home."

Sarah nodded and stepped away from the bank. Holding Ella close, she turned and slowly walked home. Before long she was parted from her precious child. But still she trusted in God.

The wise old woman's prophecy came true. Little Ella grew up strong and beautiful, and her heart was full of music. After the Civil War, when slavery was no more, she enrolled in Fisk University in Nashville, Tennessee. There she played the piano with the Fisk Jubilee Singers. They lifted their voices with the old songs, the tunes their parents and grandparents had sung when they were slaves, asking God to set them free. The land rang with the deep, stirring spirituals. Ella Sheppard and the Jubilee Singers traveled far and wide—even across the sea to Europe, where they sang before dukes, princes, and queens.

But Ella did not forget her mother. Searching and searching, at last she found Sarah. She brought her home to take care of her always. And often the loving daughter sang this old, sweet song, which she had helped to spread throughout the world.

"Swing Low, Sweet Chariot"

Swing low, sweet chariot,
Coming for to carry me home.
Swing low, sweet chariot,
Coming for to carry me home.

I looked over Jordan and what did I see,
Coming for to carry me home?
A band of angels coming after me,
Coming for to carry me home.

If you get there before I do,
Coming for to carry me home,
Tell all my friends I'm coming too,
Coming for to carry me home.

Sometimes I'm up and sometimes I'm
  down,
Coming for to carry me home,
But still my soul seems heavenly bound,
Coming for to carry me home.

Swing low, sweet chariot,
Coming for to carry me home.
Swing low, sweet chariot,
Coming for to carry me home.

Robert E. Lee
and the
Wounded Soldier

This incident happened during the Civil War, the awful struggle that divided America against itself. In the actions of a defeated Confederate general, we see the kind of honest compassion that, in Lincoln's words, helped bind up the nation's wounds.

A fierce battle had just ended at Gettysburg, Pennsylvania, the fiercest battle of the Civil War. The Union army had won a great victory, and the defeated Confederate forces were now retreating from the field.

A Union soldier lay on the ground not far from Cemetery Ridge, his leg shattered by a bullet. He hated slavery and had grown to hate Southerners during the war. He had fought them bitterly and could see nothing good in any of them. Now his pain made him hate them even more.

The stricken man saw a group of Confederate officers riding along. At their front rode a man with a straight back and snow-white beard. The soldier knew at once it was General Robert E. Lee, the enemy's leader. Anger swelled in his breast.

Though faint from fever and loss of blood, he raised his hands, looked Lee in the face, and shouted as loud as he could: "Hurrah for the Union!"

General Lee heard the mocking cry. He looked, stopped his horse, and dismounted. Slowly he walked toward the wounded man. The Union soldier shrank back, certain the Rebel general intended to kill him.

But Lee looked down with such a sad expression that at once all fear left the wounded man. He wondered what the Confederate general meant to do.

General Lee reached out and grasped the soldier's hand firmly. Looking into his eyes, he said softly, "My son, I hope you will soon be well."

The Union soldier stared back. The expression on General Lee's face was so weary and kind that he knew he would never forget it if he lived a thousand years. There he was, beaten, retiring from a field that had cost him and his army their last hope, and yet he stopped to comfort a wounded foe who had taunted him as he passed by!

General Lee rode slowly away. His words, however, lodged in the soldier's heart and stayed there long after the war ended.

Margaret of New Orleans

~ ADAPTED FROM SARAH CONE BRYANT

Throughout our history, countless people have come to this land of opportunity and receiving much, have given even more in return. Margaret Haughery was one such immigrant. Her life, modest and compelling, is a reminder that charity is among our most honored national traits.

If you ever go to beautiful New Orleans, someone might take you down to the old part of the city along the wide Mississippi River and show you a statue that stands there. It depicts a woman sitting in a low chair, with her arms around a child who leans against her. The woman is not very pretty. She wears thick shoes and a plain dress. She is stout and short, and her face is square-chinned. But her eyes look at you like your mother's.

This is the statue of a woman named Margaret. Her whole name was Margaret Haughery, but no one in New Orleans remembers her by it, any more than you would think of your sister or your best friend by her full name. She is just Margaret. Born across the ocean in Ireland more than 150 years ago, she came to America when she was just a little girl and grew up here. Her statue is one of the first ever made in our country in honor of a woman.

As a young woman Margaret was all alone in the world.
She was poor but strong, and she knew how to work. All
day, from morning until evening, she ironed clothes in a
laundry. And every day, as she worked by the window, she
saw the little children from the nearby orphanage working
and playing. They had no mothers or fathers of their own
to take care of them. Margaret knew they needed a good
friend.

You would hardly think that a poor woman who worked
in a laundry could be much of a friend to so many children.
But Margaret was. She went straight to the kind Sisters
who ran the orphanage and told them she wanted to help
the little ones.

So she gave part of her wages every week to the orphanage. She worked so hard that she was able to save some
money, too. With this, she bought two cows and a delivery
cart. She carried milk to her customers in the little cart
every morning. As she went along, she asked for leftover
food from hotels and rich houses, and brought it back in the
cart to the hungry children in the orphanage. In the very
hardest times, that was often all the food the children had.

In spite of her giving, Margaret was so careful and so
good at business that she was able to buy more cows and
earn more money. With this, she helped build a home for
orphan babies. She called it her baby house.

After a time, Margaret had a chance to take over a bakery, and then she became a bread woman instead of a milk woman. She carried the bread just as she had carried the milk, in her cart. And still she kept giving money to the orphanage.

Then a great war came, the Civil War. In all the trouble and fear of that time, Margaret drove her cart. Somehow she always had enough bread to give to the hungry soldiers and to her babies, besides what she sold. And despite all this, she earned enough so that when the war was over she built a big steam factory to make her bread.

By this time everybody in the city knew her. The children all over New Orleans loved her. The businessmen were proud of her. The poor people all came to her for advice. She used to sit at the open door of her office in a calico gown and a little shawl and give a good word to everybody, rich or poor.

Margaret grew old and, by and by, one day she died. When it was time to read her will, people found that, even with all her giving, she had still saved a great deal of money—and she had left every cent of it to the orphanages of the city. Each one of them was given something. Whether the children were boys or girls, white or black, Jews or Christians, made no difference, for Margaret always said, "They are all orphans alike." Her splendid will was signed with an *X* instead of a name, for Margaret had never learned to read or write.

The people of New Orleans said, "She was a mother to the motherless. She was a friend to those who had no friends. She had wisdom greater than schools can teach. We will not let her memory go from us." So they made a statue of her, just as she used to look sitting in her office door or driving in her own little cart. And there it stands today, in memory of the great love and the great power of plain Margaret Haughery of New Orleans.

"Home on the Range"

This song has been called the cowboy's national anthem. Here is the America of wide-open spaces and boundless optimism—the land where seldom is heard a discouraging word.

Oh, give me a home where the buffalo roam,
Where the deer and the antelope play,
Where seldom is heard a discouraging word,
And the skies are not cloudy all day.

Chorus:
Home, home on the range,
Where the deer and the antelope play,
Where seldom is heard a discouraging word,
And the skies are not cloudy all day.

Where the air is so pure, the zephyrs so free,
The breezes so balmy and light,
That I would not exchange my home on the range
For all the cities so bright.

How often at night when the heavens are bright
With the light of the glittering stars,
Have I stood here amazed and asked as I gazed
If their glory exceeds that of ours.

Oh, give me a land where the bright diamond sand
Flows leisurely down the stream,
Where the graceful white swan goes gliding along
Like a maid in a heavenly dream.

John Henry and the Steam Drill

Some say this race between man and machine really took place in the 1870s in West Virginia, although no one can say for sure. But the story and ballad of John Henry remind us of a great American tradition: pride and pleasure in work.

Folks say John Henry was born to be a steel-driving man. His twelve-pound hammer whirled round his shoulders like the wind. When it fell, it crashed like a thunderclap. When it hit steel, sparks rained like lightning.

John Henry lived in the days when something mighty big was happening in America. From coast to coast, men were building railroads—great railroads like the Union Pacific, the Illinois Central, and the Chesapeake and Ohio. John Henry helped lay the tracks. Sometimes he drove big steel spikes into the cross-ties to hold the rails in place. Other times he hammered long steel drills into rock to cut tunnels through the mountains. After he drilled a hole, the blasting crews packed it with dynamite, lit a fuse, and blew the rock to pieces.

This story takes place when the C&O Railroad was digging the Big Bend Tunnel through the high Appalachian Mountains in West Virginia. John Henry was there, driving steel faster and harder than any five men working together. His big hammer arced through the air like a rainbow. It rang like silver and shone like gold. It pealed like a hundred bells the day Captain Tommy walked up and laid a hand on John Henry's shoulder.

"John Henry," he said, "there's a man outside selling a shiny, new steam drilling machine. Says it can do the work of six men. But I say you can beat the steam drill. What do you say?"

John Henry lowered his hammer.

"Captain," he said, "I'd rather die than let that machine beat me down."

John Henry told his captain,
"A man ain't nothin' but a man,
Fo' I let that steam drill beat me down
I'll die with this hammer in my hand, Lord, Lord,
I'll die with this hammer in my hand."

And every man in that tunnel cheered.

The contest started the very next morning. The big steam drill stood on the left, gleaming and hissing and humming. John Henry stood on the right with a big twenty-pound hammer in his hand. A crowd swarmed all around.

Captain Tommy blew his whistle and the race was on.

The steam drill gave a shriek and a roar. It smashed into the mountain, gnawing rock and spitting clouds of dust.

John Henry swung his hammer with giant mountain-cracking strokes. The drill head smoked from the force of his blows. Men stood around with buckets of water to pour, trying to keep the hammer from catching fire.

After a while John Henry paused to catch his breath. He glanced at Little Bill, who held the long steel drill in place.

"How we doing, Little Bill?" he asked.

Little Bill shook his head. A frown creased his dusty brow.

"Machine's ahead, John Henry."

John Henry just laughed and swung harder. The sparks flew high as steel struck steel. His hammer burned like a torch, and the whole tunnel glowed with the flame.

"How we doing now?" John Henry yelled.

Little Bill grinned.

"Steam drill broke down," he said. "They'll have to drag it outside and fix it. Now's the time to catch up."

John Henry laughed again and drove harder.

> *John Henry told his captain,*
> *"Look yonder, what do I see?*
> *That drill's done broke, and the hole's done choke,*
> *And it can't drive steel like me, Lord, Lord,*
> *It can't drive steel like me."*

But pretty soon the steam drill was chugging and hissing again, tearing away at the rock. John Henry was driving steel, too. His hammer streaked like a meteor. The mountain rumbled with every stroke. And John Henry's heart pounded against his ribs so hard, folks say you could hear them crack.

"Time!" Captain Tommy yelled. The race was over. The judges measured the holes. John Henry had driven fifteen feet into the rock. The steam drill had gone only nine.

The crowd roared and rushed forward. But John Henry slumped against his hammer. The next minute he was on the ground.

"I beat that steam engine," he gasped, "but I broke inside."

> John Henry was hammerin' in the mountain,
> Till the handle of his hammer caught fire,
> He drove so hard that he broke his poor heart,
> Then he laid down his hammer and he died,
>   Lord, Lord,
> He laid down his hammer and he died.

They carried him outside and laid him to rest near the mouth of the tunnel with his hammer in his hand. Before long, the big new machines took over the work of the steel-driving men. But the men never stopped singing about how John Henry whipped that steam drill. And they say that if he were alive today, he'd beat any other machine that came along, too.

> They took John Henry to the tunnel,
> And they buried him in the sand,
> An' every locomotive come rollin' by
> Says, "There lies a steel-drivin' man, Lord, Lord,
> There lies a steel-drivin' man."

"The New Colossus"

— EMMA LAZARUS

Poet and patriot Emma Lazarus worked tirelessly to aid the thousands of Jewish refugees who flocked to America in the 1880s after suffering terrible persecution in Russia. Years later, her now-famous poem was engraved on the base of the Statue of Liberty. Its title refers to the Colossus of Rhodes, one of the seven wonders of the ancient world, a giant bronze statue that overlooked the Greek city's harbor. These verses remind us that America is the world's brightest beacon of freedom and hope.

Not like the brazen giant of Greek fame,
With conquering limbs astride from land to land;
Here at our sea-washed, sunset gates shall stand
A mighty woman with a torch, whose flame
Is the imprisoned lightning, and her name
Mother of Exiles. From her beacon-hand
Glows world-wide welcome; her mild eyes command
The air-bridged harbor that twin cities frame.

"Keep, ancient lands, your storied pomp!" cries she
With silent lips. "Give me your tired, your poor,
Your huddled masses yearning to breathe free,
The wretched refuse of your teeming shore,
Send these, the homeless, tempest-tost to me:
I lift my lamp beside the golden door."

The Wizard of Menlo Park

One night in 1914 an awful fire roared through one of Thomas Edison's factories in West Orange, New Jersey. By morning all seemed lost. "We've just cleared out a bunch of old rubbish," Edison insisted. "We'll build it back bigger and better." That sort of can-do attitude made Edison an ingenious inventor. And it has made American invention and industry the greatest in the world.

Thomas Alva Edison was a curious boy. He was always poking and prodding to find out how things worked and asking all sorts of questions. Why is the sky blue? Why does the wind blow? Why do bees buzz?

"Why shouldn't people be able to fly like birds?" he asked himself. So he set about trying to figure out a way.

Thomas's laboratory was in the basement of the Edison house in Port Huron, Michigan. There he collected old jars, wires, chemicals, and scraps of metal to perform his experiments. His eye lit upon a bottle of Seidlitz powder, a popular medicine in those days. Mix a little powder in a glass of water and you got lots of dancing bubbles.

"All you have to do is fill your stomach with these bubbles and you'll float like a balloon," Thomas thought. That was it!

As good as the idea was, Thomas was not about to try it on himself. So now he needed a volunteer for his experiment. In the backyard he found his friend Michael Oates. Thomas carefully explained his plan.

"Fly? Who wants to fly?" Michael frowned. "Besides, how am I gonna get down?"

Thomas had already thought of that.

"Just grab hold of those tree branches as you go floating by," he instructed. "I'll run and get a ladder and haul you back to earth."

Michael was willing. He took a deep breath, threw his head back, and gulped down a big dose.

The two boys stood blinking and waiting.

"Flap your arms!" Thomas yelled.

Michael flapped.

"Jump!"

Michael was looking a little light-headed. He wobbled. He hiccuped.

He dropped like a stone.

Michael Oates got a stomachache. Thomas got a switching.

But he never gave up asking questions and trying to find answers. When he grew up, he built a laboratory in Menlo Park, New Jersey, and brought together a team of swift-minded men to help him in his experiments. It was the world's very first "invention factory"—a business devoted to dreaming up and testing useful devices.

Before long he invented a machine that made him famous all over the world. He drew a sketch of his idea on a piece of paper and gave it to the men in the lab to make. They shook their heads in doubt but carefully built the machine and brought it to his desk. As they crowded around, he turned the machine's crank and shouted a nursery rhyme: "Mary had a little lamb. Its fleece was white as snow. . . ."

Then he turned the crank again, and all the men jumped back when they heard the same voice coming out of the machine: "Mary had a little lamb. . . ."

Thomas Edison had invented the phonograph. For the very first time, the world could record and play back sounds.

Most of his inventions did not come so quickly, though. Almost always he had to try and try again. One time he conducted experiment after experiment without finding the answer he needed. A friend said he was sorry the tests were failing.

"We haven't failed." Edison smiled. "Now we know a thousand things that won't work, so we're that much closer to finding what will."

His most important invention came that way—by trying again and again. In those days, homes were lit by candles or gas lamps. But Edison knew there must be a way to make a better source of light. He spent a year testing and searching. He tried experiment after experiment. Then one day he ran an electric current through a thin thread of baked cotton inside a glass bulb. The lamp gleamed one hour, then two—then into the night. Thomas stayed up until sunrise, watching the little lightbulb glow. He knew the world would change forever after that night. The age of electric light had dawned.

Soon people began calling Thomas Edison the Wizard of Menlo Park.

Thomas just laughed. Wizard? No, it was just plain hard work that led to such marvelous inventions. "Genius is one percent inspiration and ninety-nine percent perspiration," he said.

Edison spent many more years improving his lightbulb and thinking of ways to carry electricity to lamps in homes, offices, factories, and streets. Over the course of his life he came up with more than 1,000 inventions. He created different kinds of batteries, methods to manufacture chemicals, and a way to make the telephone better. He even invented a machine to show moving pictures, thereby helping to found one of America's most famous industries: the movies.

Thomas Edison went on working, testing, and inventing all his life. Even as an old man, he kept searching for answers to his questions. "I am long on ideas, but short on time," he said. When he died in 1931 at the age of eighty-four, lights were dimmed all across the country to honor the Wizard of Menlo Park, the greatest of all American inventors.

Martin Luther King's Dream

This is the story of one of our greatest spokesmen for freedom, a man who reminded Americans that all of God's children are created equal.

Martin Luther King, Jr., liked going to church when he was a boy in Atlanta, Georgia. His father was the minister there, and his mother led the choir. Martin's favorite hymn was called "I Want to Be More and More Like Jesus." He loved singing it while his mother played the organ. And he loved listening to the big words his father used when he preached from behind the pulpit.

"When I grow up, I'm going to get some big words, too," he used to say.

Home was just three blocks away in a big wooden house on Auburn Avenue. Martin felt happy and safe there. Every morning began with a prayer, and every evening the family was together for supper. Around the dinner table, Mr. and Mrs. King taught their children the important lessons of life. Above all, they taught Martin and his brother and sister to do unto others as you would have them do unto you.

But not everyone lived according to that rule, as Martin found out when he turned six. That was the year he started school.

Two of Martin's good friends were white boys. Martin went to one school where all the children were black, and his two friends went to another school where all the boys and girls were white. After school, Martin ran to see his friends. But when he knocked on their doors, their mothers said his friends could not come out and play with Martin anymore.

"But why?" asked Martin.

"Because we are white, and you are black," came the answer.

Martin ran home to ask his mother why he could not play with his friends. She took him into her lap and told him how black people had once been slaves, and how Abraham Lincoln had freed the slaves in the Civil War. But in many ways black people still were not free, she explained, because there were laws to keep them from doing all the things white people could do. In the South, black people could not go to the same schools as white people. They could not eat at the same restaurants. Black children could not play in the parks white children played in or drink from the same water fountains. Blacks were kept out of many jobs, and in many places they were not given the chance to vote on election day.

It was hard for Martin to understand how there could be such laws. But he knew they were wrong. He told himself that someday he would try to change them.

Martin studied hard as he grew up. He liked words and books and the great ideas they could teach. At college, he decided to become a minister like his father and grand-father. That way he could help people be kind and fair toward each other, just as Jesus wanted. Night after night, he pored over the works of great thinkers and writers, soaking up their wisdom, and seeking answers about how to serve God and his fellow man.

After school, Martin moved to Montgomery, Alabama, with his new wife, Coretta, whom he had met in college. There Martin began his career as a preacher at a Baptist church, and there he found his chance to help change the laws that kept black and white people apart.

When black people in Montgomery wanted to ride a bus, they had to sit in the back, in a special section. And if the bus was full, the law said that the black riders must stand and give their seats to white people.

One day a black woman named Rosa Parks was riding on a bus. The bus grew crowded, and the driver told her to give her seat to a white man. But Rosa Parks was tired from working all day. And she was tired of being pushed around. She refused to give up her seat. The next thing she knew, she was under arrest.

Word of what happened spread quickly. All the black people of Montgomery were tired of being pushed around.

So Reverend King and the other black leaders came up with a daring plan. They asked the city's black people to stop riding the buses. And they began to speak out against the kind of evil laws that forced blacks to the back of the bus. It was a brave and dangerous stand. But Reverend King and his friends would not be frightened out of doing what was right. They stayed off the buses until the blacks could ride side by side with whites.

But there were still many other laws in many cities and states which treated black people unfairly. So Reverend King set about trying to change them, too. Across the South, he gave speeches saying that in the eyes of the law, all people should be treated as equals. He spoke in a rich, deep voice that made people stop and listen. Now he put to use all of those beautiful, powerful words he had read and studied. He used them to make people think about how they should treat one another. He told them he was speaking out because he loved America deeply and wanted all of its citizens to be free.

Again and again, Reverend King paid a heavy price. He received ugly letters in the mail and threatening phone calls in the middle of the night. Many times he was thrown into dark, lonely jails for giving his speeches and leading protests. Sometimes his heart sank, and he grew discouraged. But whenever he thought of quitting, it seemed as though he could hear the voice of Jesus saying, "Stand up for what is right. Stand up for truth. I will be with you."

One summer day in 1963, thousands and thousands of Americans gathered in Washington, D.C. Black and white people came from all over the country to call for a nation where the laws would treat all people as equals. They marched peacefully to the Lincoln Memorial, where Reverend King stood before them and spoke.

"I have a dream," he told the great crowd. "It is a dream deeply rooted in the American dream. I have a dream that one day little black boys and black girls will be able to join hands with little white boys and white girls and walk together as sisters and brothers. I have a dream today."

As the nation listened to Reverend King, people realized that the words he spoke were what America is all about: freedom and equality for all men and women, no matter the color of their skin. They realized that Americans need to live together, not apart. Across the country, more and more people both black and white joined Reverend King in his cause. As time passed, minds began to change. And slowly the laws began to change, too.

Then something tragic happened. In 1968, Reverend King traveled to Memphis, Tennessee, to help some workers get more pay. He was standing on his motel balcony, talking to some friends, when a gunshot sounded. Reverend King collapsed on the floor. In one brief instant, the man who helped millions of Americans find hope and courage was taken away, and the country mourned.

But Reverend King's dream did not die. Instead, people drew strength from his example and his words. Remembering his bravery, black and white people kept striving to make our country a place where everyone can work together, learn together, and pray together. They labor still to make it a nation where people of all races can sit down at the table of brotherhood together. Today all of us want the America of Reverend King's dream—an America where freedom rings for every citizen all across the land.

The *Eagle* Has Landed

Curiosity about the unknown led early voyagers to our shores. They called it the New World back then. Nearly five hundred years later, that same spirit led Americans to a more distant world—the moon.

It was one of humankind's oldest dreams. For hundreds of years, people had looked to the sky and wondered if they would ever walk on the moon.

"Never." Some shook their heads. "It can't be done."

"Someday," the dreamers insisted.

One July morning in 1969, three Americans, named Neil Armstrong, Mike Collins, and Buzz Aldrin, climbed into a tiny space capsule atop a giant rocket and waited for a countdown. Five huge engines thundered to life. Flames and smoke poured across the launchpad and Apollo 11 rode a column of fire into the sky.

"We have liftoff!" announced a voice on the ground.

No one knew if the men on board would ever make it back.

Gazing down, the astronauts saw the wide curve of the Earth with its spreading seas and lush forests and drifting clouds. Through the capsule's window, they watched their planet shrink into a blue and white sphere. The spaceship rolled and the Earth slipped silently out of sight.

For three days, the Apollo 11 astronauts hurtled into the blackness of space. A second sphere, this one gray and lifeless, swelled until it filled their window. Then they were circling the moon.

Neil Armstrong and Buzz Aldrin squeezed through a hatch and crawled into a boxy, four-legged landing vehicle named the *Eagle*. In this fragile craft they would try to drop to the moon's surface while Mike Collins flew high above, ready to rescue his friends if anything went wrong.

The radio hissed and crackled. A voice called from Mission Control in Houston, Texas, a quarter million miles away, "You are go for separation."

Slowly the *Eagle* and the mother ship backed away from each other. The lander floated free.

"The *Eagle* has wings," Neil Armstrong reported to Earth. Inside the cramped cabin, he and Aldrin watched the ghostly moonscape rolling by.

Everything was ready. Another order came from Houston. "You are go for powered descent."

The engine fired and the *Eagle* began its short downward journey. Armstrong nodded and Aldrin grinned to himself. They were going to land on the moon.

But suddenly bells began to clang inside the tiny craft. Something was wrong.

"Give us a reading on that alarm," Armstrong called back to Earth. His voice was suddenly strained. If it was a serious problem, they would have to turn back.

"Hang tight," came the instruction.

The *Eagle's* computer, which was guiding the ship, had signaled that it was having trouble handling all its chores. The astronauts' hearts thumped hard inside their chests. The gray face of the moon rushed toward them. There was nothing to do but wait for Houston to study the problem and tell them whether to keep going or abandon the mission.

Then came the command. "*Eagle*, you are go for landing. Go!"

The spacecraft continued downward.

Armstrong turned to the window to look for their landing zone. He did not like what he saw. They were not where they were supposed to be.

The computer was programmed to steer the ship to a flat, smooth place for a landing. But it had overshot its target. They were plunging straight toward an area littered with deadly rocks and craters.

A light blinked on the control panel. They were running out of landing fuel.

There was no time to waste. Armstrong gripped the hand controller and took command from the computer. He had to find a place where they could set down, fast, or they would have to fire their rockets and return to space.

Gently he brought the *Eagle* under his control. The lander hovered as Armstrong searched the ground below for a level spot.

"Sixty seconds," the voice from Mission Control warned.

Sixty seconds of fuel left.

Balanced on a cone of fire, the *Eagle* scooted over rocky ridges and yawning craters.

There was no place to land!

"Thirty seconds!"

Now there was no turning back. If the engines gulped the last of the landing fuel, there would be no time to fire the rockets that could take them back into orbit. They would crash.

The landing craft swooped across boulder fields as its pilot hunted, judged, and committed. Flames shot down as the *Eagle* dropped the last few feet. Dust that had lain still for a billion years flew up and swallowed the craft.

Back on Earth, millions of people held their breaths and waited. They prayed and listened.

Then Neil Armstrong's faint voice came crackling across the gulf of space. "Houston, Tranquillity Base here. The *Eagle* has landed."

In a short while a hatch on the lander opened. A man in a bulky space suit backed down nine rungs of a ladder and placed his foot on the gray lunar soil. People all over the world watched the fuzzy black-and-white images on their television screens. They leaned toward their sets to catch the first words spoken by Neil Armstrong from the surface of the moon.

"That's one small step for man, one giant leap for mankind."

A few minutes later Buzz Aldrin crawled out of the *Eagle* to join his comrade. Together the astronauts planted a flag.

It would never flap in a breeze on the airless moon, so a stiff wire held it out from its pole. Aldrin stepped back and saluted the Stars and Stripes.

America had made the age-old dream come true. When they departed, our astronauts left behind a plaque that will always remain. Its words proclaim:

HERE MEN FROM THE PLANET EARTH

FIRST SET FOOT UPON THE MOON

JULY, 1969 A.D.

WE CAME IN PEACE FOR ALL MANKIND

"America"

~ SAMUEL FRANCIS SMITH

A young man named Samuel Francis Smith penned America *in 1831 while he was studying to become a minister. "Let music swell the breeze," he wrote. Listen and you can hear sweet freedom's song indeed—God's American choir lifting their voices all across this great land.*

My country 'tis of thee
Sweet land of liberty,
  Of thee I sing.
Land where my fathers died
Land of the Pilgrims' pride
From every mountainside
  Let freedom ring.

My native country, thee,
Land of the noble free
   Thy name I love.
I love thy rocks and rills
Thy woods and templed hills
My heart with rapture thrills
   Like that above.

Let music swell the breeze
And ring from all the trees
   Sweet freedom's song.
Let mortal tongues awake
Let all that breathe partake
Let rocks their silence break
   The sound prolong.

Our fathers' God, to thee,
Author of liberty
   To thee we sing.
Long may our land be bright
With freedom's holy light
Protect us by thy might
   Great God, our King.